D0933757

Published by Creative Education
P.O. Box 227, Mankato, Minnesota 56002
Creative Education is an imprint of
The Creative Company
www.thecreativecompany.us

Design and production by The Design Lab
Art direction by Rita Marshall
Printed by Corporate Graphics in the
United States of America

Photographs by Alamy (Rolf Nussbaumer Photogra-
phy), Dreamstime (Michael Lynch, Worldfoto), Getty
Images (Bruce Dale/National Geographic, Mattias
Klum, Roy Toft, WIN-Initiative), iStockphoto (George
Burba, Craig Dingle, Tom Grundy, Eric Isselée,
Valeriy Kirsanov, Mark Kostich, Michael Rolands)

Copyright © 2012 Creative Education
International copyright reserved in all countries.
No part of this book may be reproduced in any
form without written permission from the publisher.

Library of Congress Cataloging-in-Publication Data
Riggs, Kate.
Bats / by Kate Riggs.
p. cm. — (Amazing animals)
Summary: A basic exploration of the appearance,
behavior, and habitat of bats, Earth's only flying
mammals. Also included is a story from folklore
explaining how bats helped shape the earth.
Includes bibliographical references and index.
ISBN 978-1-60818-105-6
1. Bats—Juvenile literature. I. Title. II. Series.
QL737.C5R484 2012
599.4—dc22   2010049117

CPSIA: 042412 PO1568

9 8 7 6 5 4 3

Riggs, Kate.
Bats /

c2012.
33305225536444
sa   09/21/12

NG ANIMALS

BATS

BY KATE RIGGS

CREATIVE ● EDUCATION

Bats use their strong wings to fly

Bats are **mammals** that fly. There are about 1,000 kinds of bats. They live all over the world. Most bats live in really warm places.

mammals animals that have hair or fur and feed their babies with milk

All bats have two wings and small hind feet. Their bodies are covered with soft fur. Some bats are yellow, gray, or even bright orange. But most bats are black or brown.

*Vampire bats have fur
that is gray or brown*

The biggest bats in the world are giant golden-crowned fruit bats. They weigh up to three pounds (1.4 kg). Their wings stretch more than five feet (1.5 m) across! Philippine bamboo bats are the smallest bats. They are only 1.5 inches (3.8 cm) long.

The Indian flying fox is a kind of big fruit bat

*Some bats move into
caves to hibernate*

There are two groups of bats, megabats and microbats. Many megabats live in warm places like rainforests. Microbats like heat, too, but they can also live in cooler areas. They **hibernate** when it gets too cold.

hibernate spend the winter in one place, sleeping most of the time, without going outside

Bats that eat blood (left) or nectar (opposite) have long tongues

Megabats eat fruit. Some eat **nectar** from flowers, too. Some microbats, like vampire bats, eat blood from animals. Other microbats eat insects, frogs, birds, and sometimes fish.

nectar a sugary liquid made by plants

Most mother bats have one **pup** each year. Newborn microbats are blind and hairless. Megabats are born with their eyes open and have fur. Pups drink their mother's milk to grow strong. They start flying when they are two to four weeks old. Many bats live for 20 years or more.

pup a baby bat

Bats hang upside down so they are always ready to fly

Bats are nocturnal (*nahk-TER-nuhl*) animals. This means that they sleep in the daytime and are awake at night. Bats **roost** upside down in trees or caves during the day. They fly around at night. This is when they find food.

roost come together with other bats to sleep

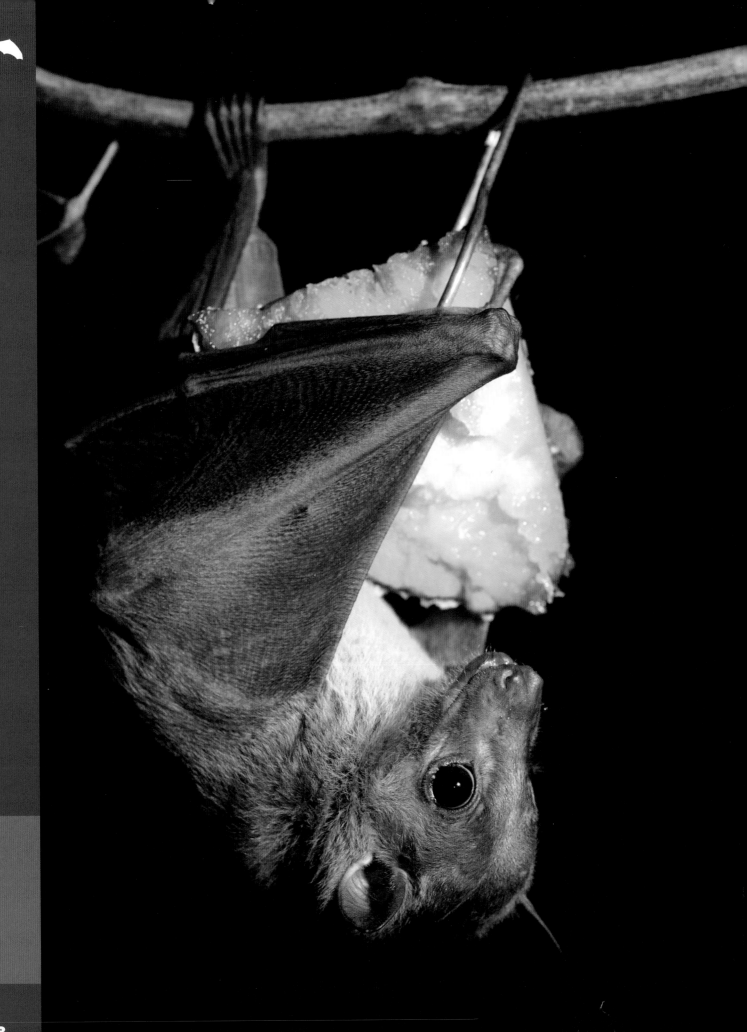

Brightly colored fruit is ripe, or ready to eat

Megabats can see colors.

This helps them find fruits that are good to eat. Microbats find food through **echolocation** (*EK-oh-loh-KAY-shun*). They can tell when **prey** is close by. Then they swoop in and catch it.

echolocation finding things by sensing their sound and shape

prey animals that are killed and eaten by other animals

People can see bats in caves. Thousands of Mexican free-tailed bats live in Carlsbad Caverns National Park in New Mexico. Other people can see bats near their homes. It is exciting to see these winged animals fly through the night!

Bats live in many caves around the U.S.

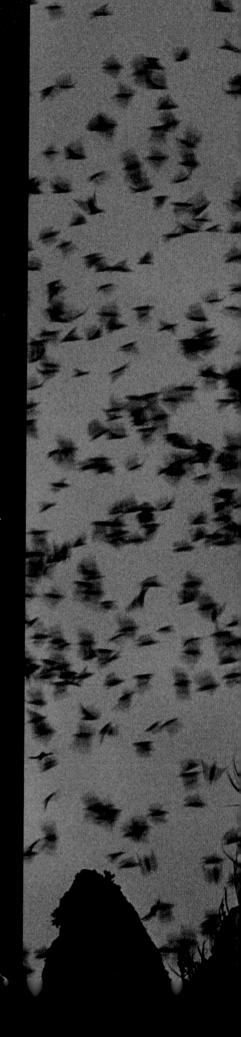

A *Bat Story*

Why are some parts of land hilly and others flat? People in Mexico used to tell a story about how bats helped shape the earth. Long ago, the earth was flat. When it rained, the water made big puddles all over the land. The people asked Bat to fly over the land and scoop valleys and **mountains** out of it. Bat did so, and the people were happy with the land from then on.

mountains very big hills made of rock

Read More

Earle, Ann. *Zipping, Zapping, Zooming Bats*. New York: HarperCollins, 1995.

Morris, Ting. *Bat*. North Mankato, Minn.: Smart Apple Media, 2006.

Web Sites

Enchanted Learning: Bats
http://www.enchantedlearning.com/subjects/mammals/bat/shapebook/
This site has printouts that can be made into a book about bats.

Bats 4 Kids: Bat Page Game Room
http://www.bats4kids.org/gamesite.htm
This site has bat facts and games to play.

Index